Girlfriend Gatherings

Janet Holm McHenry

HARVEST HOUSE PUBLISHERS
Eugene, Oregon 97402

Girlfriend Gatherings

Copyright © 2001 by Janet Holm McHenry
Published by Harvest House Publishers
Eugene, Oregon 97402

McHenry, Janet Holm.
  Girlfriend gatherings / Janet Holm McHenry.
    p. cm.
  Includes bibliographical references.
  ISBN 0-7369-0593-6
  1. Christian women—Religious life. 2. Friendship—Religious aspects—Christianity. I. Title.

BV4527 .M3925 2001
248.8'43—dc21   2001016901

Published in association with the literary agency of *Janet Kobobel Grant, Books & Such, 3093 Maiden Lane, Altadena, California 91001.*

Cover by Left Coast Design, Portland, Oregon

Design and production by Matthew Shoemaker

Harvest House Publishers has made every effort to trace the ownership of all poems and quotes. In the event of a question arising from the use of a poem or quote, we regret any error made and will be pleased to make the necessary correction in future editions of this book.

Poor Man's Cookies recipe used with permission by Mary Pielenz Hampton from her book, *A Tea for All Seasons*, Grand Rapids: Zondervan, 1977.

Unless otherwise indicated, Scripture quotations are taken from the Holy Bible, New International Version®, Copyright © 1973, 1978, 1984 by the International Bible Society. Used by permission of Zondervan Publishing House. Scripture quotations marked TLB are from The Living Bible Copyright © 1971. Used by permission of Tyndale House Publishers, Inc., Wheaton, Illinois 60189. All rights reserved. Scripture quotations marked NKJV are taken from the New King James Version. Copyright ©1982 by Thomas Nelson, Inc. Used by permission. All rights reserved.

Printed in the United States of America.

01 02 03 04 05 06 07 08 09 / DC-MS / 10 9 8 7 6 5 4 3 2 1

To all the girlfriends of my life:
thanks for listening, giving, loving.

In memory of Rose Roberti,
who showed us faith, courage, and compassion.

Contents

*Never
abandon
a friend...*

Proverbs 27:10 (TLB)

Cultivating Friendships

When summer began, I took a long look at my dismal perennial garden in my backyard. The white roses that were supposed to grow in my almost-mile-high mountain valley were crispy. The lavender, which I had planted to sweeten the air, was nonaromatic. The lilies were wilting. And the spiked purple thingies (I'm not too good with names) were purpleless. However, the crabgrass was doing very well. It was all my fault, really. I had not watered the flowers, fed them, or nurtured them by weeding. And they were dying because of my lack of care. I decided to get down on my knees. Yes, a few prayers helped, but mostly it was the watering, the feeding, and the weeding that brought them back to life.

A few weeks later I was enjoying their beauty and aroma while I opened my mail on my back deck. Nestled among the bills was an announcement of my husband's and my 30th high school reunion later that summer. As I read through the list of missing graduates the committee wanted to find, I wondered about the lives of my large circle of high school friends. Most of us dozen or more ladies had lost touch. Our friendship circle, it seemed to me, had become a neglected garden.

As I read some of their names, I decided my friends were still important to me. They were the young women who warmly welcomed a shy girl from the East coast in her sophomore year in a new school. Without my connection to them, those years of my life would have been without much meaning.

But you move on…and on…and on…and start over… and over…and over. And it's hard to make new friends and even harder to keep in touch with the others. For a while I wondered if there were simply seasons for friends. Perhaps my high school friends were Spring Girlfriends. And if my college and young adult friends were Summer Girlfriends, maybe now I was falling into a season of Autumn Girlfriends.

I was okay with that philosophy until I realized that I truly missed my friends of the past and longed for ways to stay in touch. By the time I had gotten the reunion announcement, I had decided I wanted to actively seek ways to stay connected with friends from all of my life's seasons.

Girlfriend Gatherings is the product of that search, as I've found some treasures to share with you. First, I'd like to share some stories about special ladies who have made a difference in my life and in the lives of others. You'll learn how they met and how they have stayed connected over the years. Each chapter will help you think about the different kinds of relationships you can have—at work, at home, between generations, with neighbors, and more. Or, perhaps you'll be inspired to seek out long lost friends and make a connection.

Each chapter will also offer easy-to-follow sidebars with practical suggestions for keeping in touch, whether you're working in the home or at a job. And hey, I know you're busy. I've got four kids and two jobs myself! I've had to find simple ways to get together with friends. So, I'm hoping you'll find my ideas convenient and easy to slip into your life here and there.

Whatever form your gatherings take, I assure you, they'll add a sweet fragrance to the seasons of your life. Happy gathering!

Gathering High School Friends

"Why don't we get all our friends together?"

I smiled at the e-mail message. It was from Linda, my dear friend of high school years past, and suddenly I was reminiscing about our first meeting.

I had nervously climbed up the steps and taken a seat on the yellow school bus that would leave our suburban Sacramento neighborhood and wind around country roads for an hour. I didn't know a soul on that day I would begin my first day of high school. My dad's job transfer had just moved my family from Albuquerque. Other teenagers greeted each other as they plopped into seats together. I stared out the window at nothing in particular.

"Hi. Okay if I sit here?"

I nodded as a lovely girl with straight, long blonde hair sat beside me. Maybe this was the one friend I had prayed for the night before. "I just need one friend, God, just one to walk through those big doors with."

I nervously eyed my friend sidewise, hoping she wouldn't notice my stare. And then I fixated on the most amazing things and blurted without thinking.

"You have the biggest hands I've ever seen!"

She gasped slightly. "Well, thanks! That makes *me* feel good."

I died inside. I had said the dumbest thing I had ever said in my life. I wanted to run back down the bus aisle for home. I wanted to hide in my room. I...I wanted to go anywhere

12

but Elk Grove High School on that bus sitting next to that pretty girl. I certainly hadn't meant to hurt her feelings.

I wanted to say I was sorry, but instead I bit my tongue, afraid the pools in my eyes would turn to sobs and attract the turning eyes of every single person on that bus. Had I lost the one potential friend God had sent my way?

But then she spoke. "Well, that's the craziest way to make friends, but hi, I'm Linda."

She held out her lovely model-like hand, and I met one of the best friends I would ever have. For the next three years we joined clubs together, sat on rooters' buses to games, fashioned crepe-paper flowers for homecoming floats, and critiqued boys. We dragged K Street in downtown Sacramento before it became a mall, crawled through the tule fog to basketball games, and critiqued boys. And she hosted the best pool parties at her house where we'd challenge each other to do amazingly stupid

13

tricks off her diving board, while we of course, critiqued boys. We even sang "Nearer, my God, to Thee..." and "Onward, Christian soldiers..." in Job's Daughters while wearing our angelic-looking gowns. We were the B.B.O.B.s— Bloomin' Blokes of Britain—and neither of us still probably knows what we meant by that. We just liked fun.

Later we became college roommates at UC Davis for a year, which may have been the best year of my life. I learned how to buy groceries for four for a week for only $28.00. I learned how to make lasagna and talarini and omelets. I learned how to call a doctor when you're so sick you can't even get out of bed.

And I learned how to have a personal relationship with God. That was because of Linda, too. She and a neighbor friend, Bill, coaxed me to a Sunday-evening free movie at the local theater: "For Pete's Sake." Although I had always attended church, for the first time in my life I heard that I could know God in my heart. With Linda at my side I prayed the prayer that would change my life, and we became not only friends but also Christian sisters. That night we celebrated our newfound faith over Bill's homemade bread and a sip of communion wine—a "first supper" of sorts that cemented our Forever Friendship.

I finished out my schooling at Berkeley, but Linda and I continued our walk of friendship. The fall after I graduated she walked down the church aisle as my maid of honor. The next fall I walked down the aisle as hers. Our paths separated after that, as we each moved to different states and started our families. But a few times a year we'd write. And we exchanged Christmas photos and letters and an occasional birthday present. When we were both in Sacramento, a rarity, we'd look each other up, and a few times we connected at high school reunions.

And then all of a sudden, there it was...the e-mail from Linda just a month away from our 30th reunion. How could it be? Thirty years? I joked with her that I still had way too many emotional problems to be that old. And that made me wonder: what if our other high school friends were still wrestling with some of life's junk? Could a friend be grieving the recent death of a parent, as was I? Could someone be going through a divorce? Perhaps another person was at a critical meeting of crossroads: one of our friends had committed suicide years ago. Maybe someone else right at that moment was feeling similarly lost.

And so I answered Linda's e-mail: "Yes, let's get together." And about a month later 9 of the 12 friends we were able to reach joined us in our first Girlfriend Brunch, which we have since decided will become a 5-year tradition. And yes, others were grieving the loss of parents. And several were wading through the slough of divorce. But we instantly connected that morning of our 30th reunion. And we decided that reconnecting gave us such joy and a sense of the importance of our past that we would not wait for another five years to pass. We would keep in touch through a round robin letter.

You could say that when I blurted out that dumb remark to Linda on the bus years ago, that God was "handing" me one of the most precious gifts I would ever receive: a life-long friend. With that lifelong friend I also made a connection to a whole gathering of friends who are still touching my life in significant ways. Several are clearing away debris, helping me not stumble, as I walk through the year after my dad's death. Others are cheering me as I approach the finish line of raising teenagers. In turn, I pray that I am an encouragement to them as well as they face the challenges of their lives.

17

Sir, more than kisses,
letters mingle souls;
For, thus friends
absent speak.

John Donne

Mexican Brunch for Eight

My soon-to-be son-in-law, Ozzie, is Mexican-American, and so, in his honor, I offer this easy-to-prepare brunch that will be one hot tamale with your girlfriends. Serve with hot chocolate flavored with vanilla and cinnamon; beat it until it's frothy and serve with cinnamon sticks. Yum!

Easy Chile Rellenos Casserole

Cooking spray

2 7-ounce cans whole chiles

5 cups grated Monterey Jack cheese

4 cups grated cheddar cheese

8 eggs

2 12-ounce cans evaporated milk

1/2 cup flour

1 teaspoon salt

Coat 9" x 13" baking dish with cooking spray. Layer cheeses and peppers in the dish. Beat together eggs, flour, milk, and salt; pour over cheese and peppers. Bake uncovered at 350°F for 45 minutes.

Sopapillas

2 cups flour
1 tablespoon baking powder
1/2 teaspoon salt
1 tablespoon shortening
2/3 cup lukewarm water
Oil for frying
Honey or sugar and cinnamon

Stir together flour, baking powder, and salt. Cut in the shortening until mixture feels like cornmeal. Gradually add the water, stirring with a fork (dough will be crumbly). Turn onto floured surface, kneading into a smooth ball. Divide dough in half; let stand 10 minutes. Roll each half into a 12x10-inch rectangle. Cut into small triangles, about 2 to 3 inches. Heat oil in a deep saucepan over medium heat. Fry a few at a time in the hot oil until golden. Drain on paper towels. Serve with honey or sprinkle with cinnamon sugar. Makes 40.

<u>Ensalada de Fruta</u>
1 fresh pineapple
2 large oranges
2 medium bananas
1 large apple
1 16-ounce can sliced beets, drained
1 jicama, peeled and chopped (optional)
1 stick sugar cane, peeled and chopped (optional)
Lettuce
1/2 cup peanuts, chopped
Salt
Pueblo rosea chile (crumbled fine) or chili powder
Lemon juice

Arrange lettuce leaves on a large plate or platter. Slice up fruit and arrange decoratively on lettuce. Sprinkle lightly with peanuts, salt, and chile. Liberally sprinkle with lemon juice.

Organizing a Round Robin Letter

A round robin letter is a letter that travels by regular mail on a circuit from one friend to another. It's easy to organize:

- Type a list of the names and addresses of each person on the circuit. Keep this paper clipped to the top of the other correspondence.

- Prepare your letter and attach it. Photos can be sent along, as well.

- Mail it to the person next on the list under your name.

- Each successive person writes a letter, attaches it underneath, and sends the letter to the next person on the list.

- When the originator gets the packet back, she starts a new letter and begins the round robin circuit again.

Note: It's helpful if each person on the circuit has her own address list, complete with phone numbers and e-mail addresses. This makes it easier to track down a sluggish correspondent.

Suggestion: You can make up your own alternative questionnaire or even add a list for friends to include prayer requests.

Girlfriend Musings Then and Now

<u>Yearbook then:</u>

Janet,

We've gone through high school and matured together to become ever-lasting friends, I hope. You were there to reassure me and help me on. You have been a special person to me in so many ways. Thanks for all of your help—and thanks for being my friend.

Love,

Linda

<u>Reunion now:</u>

Dear Janet,

You and I have been true lifelong friends. Even though we've had many miles between us most of the years since we've both been married, I still feel connected to you. I consider us "best friends." We're not usually able to go have coffee or lunch, but we do communicate. This e-mail has really enabled us to "talk" more often. Even though we've gone in our own directions, we can pick up from where we left off either long distance or on our occasional visits. I am blessed to have you in my life.

Love,

Linda

Yearbook then:

Dear Janet,

I'm so excited about going to Davis next year and being your "roomie"! (Are you practicing on your bike!?) It's really been lots of fun knowing you and being your friend—next year we'll continue to have good times! So long for now, "Aunt Aggie."

Happy Thots!

Katie

Reunion now:

Dear Janet,

I cried at your sweet wedding in Berkeley. I rejoiced with you and Craig at the births of your children—marveling at the striking mix of resemblance to your Holm and McHenry roots. We fluffed crepe-paper flowers for homecoming floats on warm Indian summer evenings in hay-filled barns. Now we tend flowers in our own gardens. May our years ahead blossom in the light of the Lord, "ever brighter unto the perfect day" (PROVERBS 4:18 NKJV).

Love,

Katie

24

Gathering Work Buddies

When Judy sat down at her dining room table with her friends from work, she couldn't help but notice the awkward silence. After all, there they were all sitting face-to-face when their normal posture was back-to-back. Judy worked in the composing room of a weekly newspaper, and all day long she and four other women faced the walls of a small windowless room—not each other—as they worked at their computers. On that day, they and the newspaper's editor Debra, had met at Judy's home for Christmas tea and brunch.

Despite the initial shifting of eyes and nervous smiles, the six women warmed up in the cozy atmosphere of Judy's home. They sipped hot apple cider in Christmas mugs as little teddy bears stood watch over each place around the oval oak table. Traditional carols played in the background as cinnamon and vanilla candles warmed the edges of the room, which was filled with the rest of Judy's "friends"—her collection of dozens of teddy bears.

Even though the women had never before gotten together for a social occasion, Judy knew how to make them comfortable. Several other times in years past, she had hosted young women who had worked for her in the school library—her former job—or wives of her husband's co-workers. Tall and slim with full, long brown hair and large blue eyes, Judy's smile and relaxing manner welcomed the women more than all the other surrounding comforts of her antique-filled, century-old home.

As they munched on quiche, fresh fruit salad and Finnish sweet bread with honey butter, Judy broke open the boxes of silence with her comfortable questions. Dressed in a long jumper in holiday colors and a festive matching apron, she'd ask:

"What is your favorite Christmas tradition?"

"What was your all-time favorite Christmas gift?"

"What is your fondest memory of a Christmas from your childhood?"

And one by one the women—an eclectically aged group from their 20's to 50's—relaxed, smiled and chatted about their life past, their life present and their someday hopes. After a couple hours, though, all but one left.

Alison (not her real name) lingered. "Could I help you clean up?" she asked.

27

Judy smiled. "I'd love that!" It wasn't that Judy really needed the help—there were just a few dishes. But secretly she had been hoping for a few minutes alone with Alison.

From the first day Judy had taken the job as copy editor, Alison had been a challenge. When things weren't going Alison's way at work—some editor wanted something changed or her computer bombed again—she'd cuss and yell at whoever happened to be in the way. Judy was the first copy editor ever hired at the paper, and her job meant more work for Alison. It was Judy's job to spot the typos and inconsistencies in headlines, photo cutlines, and news copy. When there were mistakes, this meant Alison and the other composing room girls had to re-do the work. And when deadlines were tight, things could be especially tough on Alison, because she did all the front and jump pages of the five weekly papers the company produced.

"She intimidated me the first couple of weeks," Judy said. "She had this gruff exterior, and I simply was afraid to tell her the pages weren't right."

But a couple months into the job their entire relationship changed. One of Judy's sons was struggling with substance abuse.

"Alison opened up when she knew of his trouble," Judy said. "It established a bridge between us."

And so the two opposites became friends. Judy was open and approachable. Alison was shy and private. Judy wore dresses and suit jackets with antique-jeweled pins on her lapels. Alison wore second-hand store Lee's jeans and T-shirts. Judy read Christian novels. Alison read romances and horse stories. Judy loved to talk on the phone with friends, but Alison could be abrupt.

Judy loved children and had enjoyed her years as an elementary school librarian. She learned that although Alison

29

had two boys of her own—in fourth and eighth grades—she really didn't like kids much. Even so, she had a fierce, mother-bear-type love for her sons.

And soon, as Judy's struggles with her own son developed, Alison became Judy's refuge at work—the one woman who had been a formidable wall! "I just think that I became more approachable when she realized that my life wasn't perfect and that I had pain and problems, too," Judy says now. "She began to wonder how I was making it through those tough times, and I'd tell her 'God is my strength.' I wouldn't preach at her, but I would give her my Christian magazines and books. And she'd read every one."

So, when the other women had left the tea that Christmas season morning, the two very different women really had a chance to talk. Judy said they talked about how hard it was raising sons, and "I told her how much I depended on God every step of the way."

And Judy felt really comfortable talking with Alison, just the two of them—Judy washing the dishes and Alison drying. Since that time, they have shared even more pain. Judy's husband left her and now she's on her way to another job in another state. And she says of any friends—from work or church or elsewhere—Alison will be one of those she'll miss the most.

I'd like to be the
sort of friend that you
have been to me;
I'd like to be the help
that you've been always
glad to be;
I'd like to mean as
much to you
each minute of the day
As you have meant,
old friend of mine,
to me along the way.

Edgar A. Guest

Hosting a High Tea on a Low Budget

High tea is served in the late afternoon and often is a substitute for dinner. Although it can be quite elegant and pricey at Victorian tea-houses, you can organize one simply and inexpensively in your own home. You don't have to buy any of the setting pieces if you don't have them; I have borrowed teapots and cloth napkins from a friend who collects them. You also don't have to buy fancy ingredients for elaborate courses. You can fix most of the following——scones, sandwiches, and cookies——from makings right in your cupboard.

The Table

Pretty tablecloth

Teapots——one for each different type of tea

Teacups——each guest can bring her own and tell a story about how she got it

Doilies (optional)——lace or paper——between the cup and saucer to catch drips

33

Tea tray

Sugar bowl and creamer

Dishes for place settings and serving of food

Silverware and cloth napkins arranged in place settings

Flowers——homegrown or otherwise

Candles

The Courses

First Course:

Tea——serve from pots——with cream (milk can substitute), sugar (cubes are great), lemon slices, and honey

Lemon-Poppy Seed Scones with Lemon Curd and butter (Scone mixes are available in the supermarket and specialty stores.)

Second Course:

More tea

Chicken-Pecan Salad Sandwiches

Tomato and Cucumber Sandwiches

Open-Faced Kiwi Sandwiches

Third Course:

Even more tea!

Poor Man's Cookies, cake, pie or fruit

Note: If you're shorter on time than money, buy cookies from the store and order the sandwiches from a deli.

Tea Recipes for Eight

<u>Lemon-Poppy Seed Scones</u>

2 cups all-purpose flour

3 teaspoons baking powder

1/4 teaspoon salt

1/4 cup sugar

1 tablespoon poppy seeds

1/3 cup butter or stick margarine

2 tablespoons bottled lemon juice

3/4 cup milk

Nonstick cooking spray

Preheat oven to 425° F. Spray cookie sheet with nonstick cooking spray. Mix flour, baking powder, salt, sugar, and poppy seeds in a large bowl. Cut in butter, using pastry blender or crisscrossing two knives, until mixture resembles fine crumbs. Mix together lemon juice and milk; stir into flour mixture until dough leaves side of bowl and forms a ball. Turn dough onto lightly floured surface; gently roll in

36

flour to coat. Knead lightly 10 times. Roll or pat into 9-inch circle. Sprinkle with sugar. Cut into 8 wedges. Place on cookie sheet. Bake 12 to 15 minutes or until golden brown. Immediately remove from cookie sheet. Serve warm. Serves 8.

Note: Instead of rolling dough into a circle, you can use a heart-shaped biscuit cutter to make individual scones.

Lemon Curd

Grated peel of 2 lemons

Juice of 2 lemons or 1/2 cup lemon juice

2 eggs, beaten

1/2 cup butter

2 cups sugar

Boil water in the bottom section of a double boiler. In the top of a double boiler, combine the lemon peel, lemon juice, eggs, butter, and sugar and stir until sugar is dissolved. Cook and stir occasionally until thick and smooth. Pour into a clean container and refrigerate after cooling. Makes one cup. Serves 8.

Chicken and Pecan Salad Sandwiches

4 to 8 slices of sandwich-style wheat bread

2 cups finely chopped, cooked chicken

1 cup finely chopped celery

1/2 cup chopped pecans

1/2 cup (or more to taste) mayonnaise

Mix above ingredients two hours ahead; then spread liberally on 4 bread slices. Can be left open-faced or topped with another slice. Open-faced sandwiches can be decorated with a slice of a grape. Cut off crusts and cut sandwiches corner-to-corner.

Tomato and Cucumber Sandwiches

8 slices sandwich-style white bread

1 medium cucumber, peeled and sliced thinly

4 ripe Italian tomatoes, sliced thinly

Mayonnaise

One hour ahead, spread mayonnaise liberally on each bread slice.
Put four slices of cucumber and four of tomato on each sandwich.
Top with another slice of bread. Trim crusts. Cut in square quarters.
Keep chilled.

Note: These can also be made open-faced.

Open-Faced Kiwi Sandwiches

1 loaf sliced party deli rye bread

8 ounces pineapple-flavored cream cheese

6 kiwi, peeled and sliced thinly

1 pint fresh strawberries (or frozen if out of season), halved

Spread cream cheese on rye bread slices. Top with kiwi slice and half
a strawberry.

Poor Man's Cookies

3 eggs

1/4 cup milk

1/4 cup sugar

2 3/4 cups flour

1/2 teaspoon salt

Vegetable oil for frying

Confectioners' sugar for dusting

In large bowl, beat eggs, milk, sugar, and salt together. Gradually blend in flour to form soft dough. Pour dough onto waxed paper, cover and refrigerate for 30 minutes. When chilled, roll dough into a 1/4-inch thick rectangle. With pastry cutter or sharp knife, cut into 3-inch squares. Cut a slash diagonally across each square. Carefully pull one corner through the slash. Repeat until all dough is used. In a deep-fat fryer or heavy, deep-sided pan, heat about 2 inches of oil to 375°F. Fry dough twists a few at a time for 1 to 2 minutes, until golden. Turn once or twice to brown on both sides. Drain twists on double thickness of paper towels. When cool, sprinkle with confectioners' sugar.

❀ Fun Resources for a Tea Party

If Teacups Could Talk by Emilie Barnes (Harvest House)

An Invitation to Tea by Emilie Barnes (Harvest House)

The Twelve Teas of Christmas by Emilie Barnes (Harvest House)

Tea and Inspiration: A Collection of Tea Celebrations to Share with Your Lord and Your Loved Ones by Mary Pielenz Hampton (Thomas Nelson)

A Tea for All Seasons by Mary Pielenz Hampton (Zondervan)

Coffee, Cookies and Inspiration: Heartwarming Moments with God by Mary Pielenz Hampton (Zondervan)

Simply Scones: Quick and Easy Recipes by Leslie Weiner and Barbara Albright (St. Martin's Press)

Make a Perpetual Date

Laurie and Jacki, although a generation apart in ages, became good friends at the large drugstore where they worked. Their friendship grew even closer when Laurie's marriage dissolved. Jacki's husband was often out of town for weeks at a time on business, so the two ladies made a standing date. Every Sunday afternoon they'd go to a chick flick together. Eventually Laurie was transferred with the company to a different location, but they'd still meet at the movies.

You may not be able to meet your friend every week, but perhaps you could make a monthly or yearly date. Meet the first time for dinner or the movies. Before the evening is over, get out your calendars and set the next time and place. Touch base a week or so beforehand to confirm the date. Agree to go dutch or alternate. Easy!

Gathering Family

I grew up in a family that thought singing together was natural. We'd take evening and weekend drives on upstate New York country roads. Dad, behind the station wagon wheel, would sing melody in bass, and Mom would harmonize in alto. We five kids would sing along to the oldies. I mean, what else was there to do, except fight? And besides, we had learned singing was fun.

When we get together, we sing. Mom will sit down at the piano and play and gradually we adults will chime in to one of the two Fieg family songs, "Oh, don't you remember sweet Betsy from Pike...." That was Pike County, Pennsylvania, most certainly, all Fiegs will claim, even though there are many counties called Pike in various states. But that's what Aunt Millie said, and whatever Aunt Millie said was gospel.

My great-aunt and the matriarch of the Fieg family, Emilie Case made a party happen. It wasn't necessarily her food down on the farm in northeast Pennsylvania, because my husband Craig still says she served him "mystery meat" one night (turkey soufflé?). It was her stories. Young and old alike would crowd around her and listen to her tales of teaching in the one-room schoolhouse down the road, of receiving letters from President Kennedy or some famous author, and of hitchhiking to her job at the library in town, a dozen miles away. She had lost her driver's license some years ago because of her cataracts but continued to work at the library into her 80's.

It was Aunt Millie who got my dad using the cassette recorder. At a family reunion in Pennsylvania after dinner one night, she got started into the stories again, with my mom's urgings as interviewer. This time it was about some of the harder times. The three-week voyage from Germany to New York as a four-year-old and her older sister Martha seasick the whole time in the upper berth. The old farmhouse in Shocopee, Pennsylvania, built like a crazy quilt with torn apart wooden food boxes. The week her mother left the six children at home to care for her sick husband in New York and only having apples and potatoes to eat the whole time.

"One day we would cook apples. The next day we'd cook potatoes. The next day we'd cook apples and potatoes and put them together. The next day we'd try to make a variety." And she'd laugh.

I haven't attended a Fieg family reunion since I was a teenager. But my extended family is now big enough to hold

45

its own in California, with about 30 of us, plus assorted boyfriends and girlfriends. It's really similar to a reunion on the farm or at the Delaware River, with kids running all over. And traditional games. And lots of storytelling going on. And probably some mystery meat.

In fact, I think Aunt Millie passed along her wordsmith gift in a crisscross fashion throughout what is now my extended family, especially to the women—Mom (her niece), my sisters, sisters-in-law, daughters, nieces. Perhaps we women are just better communicators in general. I think it's lovely that when we meet for special times together, we often share our reminiscences together through all kinds of language—songs we write, plays, poems, stories. I even wrote a rap once. That was a mini-history of my dad's life for his 70th birthday. I recruited my siblings and some of our kids, and we sagged our pants and wore baseball hats back-wards and bumped to the beat.

So instead of one central storyteller, we have many now. And it may not always be a cassette recorder we pass around; we may be staring at the lens of a video camera as we speak or sing. And all it takes is for someone to start, "I remember…" And a couple hours later we're crying and laughing and hugging. And wondering when the next magical get-together will be.

And we still sing the other Fieg song:

Down on the farm they all ask for you.
Down on the farm they all ask for you.
Down on the farm they all ask for you.
The cows ask, the pigs ask, the horses ask—
They all ask for you.

P.S. And Craig is always glad the meat is not a mystery.

For there is no
friend like a sister
In calm or stormy weather;
To cheer one on the tedious way,
To fetch one if one goes astray,
To lift one if one totters down,
To strengthen whilst one stands.

Christina Rosetti

How to Karaoke...
Even Without a Machine

A karaoke machine is a glorified cassette or CD player with a microphone. The machine usually can be wired with accessories to a television lyrics display. This equipment starts in price at something under $150 to buy; used equipment is available for sale on the Internet or in your newspaper's classifieds. If you want a cheaper alternative, check out the following, in descending order of cost:

Look for Christmas karaoke packages, sold in major warehouse stores during the holiday season——complete with 50 or more carols.

Cost: $100

Rent the equipment. Check your yellow pages under Music Equipment, Sound Systems, Rental Service or Disc Jockeys.

Cost: $60 or more

Buy a microphone and hook it into your CD or cassette player.

Cost: $50 or more

Buy your kid a Fisher-Price or other child cassette or CD player that comes with a microphone that projects sound through the speaker.

Cost: $30

Pay a teenager to set up a sound system with microphone.

Cost: $?

Pass around a wooden spoon covered in foil and improvise with sheet music or hymnals.

Cost: $0

One-Liner Story Starters

If you prefer storytelling to musical fun, here are some open-ended starters that will get people reminiscing or telling tales:

"The best vacation we ever took was..."

"The dumbest thing I ever did was..."

"My favorite class in school was...because..."

"The funniest thing I remember was when..."

"The first car I ever owned was..." (Then see if each person can name all the cars they've owned, in order.)

"I've always wanted to..."

"When the new millennium started, I was..."

"When I graduated from high school, my dream was to..."

"The biggest turning point in my life was when..."

"The person who has most helped or inspired me is... because..."

Bits of Oral History...
with Aunt Millie

When you and the women in your family get together, gather around a tape recorder and tell stories. Start with the oldest member of the group and interview her. Each person around the table can take turns asking questions. You'll find you have priceless gems—the beginnings of an oral history for your own family.

The following are bits from an interview of my Great-Aunt Millie that my mother recorded at a family reunion in 1981. Millie died three years later at age 89, the last of that generation of the Fieg/Baylor family that emigrated from Germany in 1899.

On the voyage: "It was the first time Max, your father, ever ate a banana. He thought it was an overripe cucumber!"

On leaving Germany: "It was hard times. A jewelry business was the luxury business. (My father) went bankrupt, and he went to America. He fled, I guess.

"I still have the feather bed that my mother brought from Germany...the dog is sleeping on it now. I'm afraid it's got fleas in it."

On moving to the farm: "My mother would go to the theater whenever she could. And when we came up there to Shocopee, it was tragedy for her on that lonesome little old farm with no amusements or no friends."

On love and marriage: "(Brother Lothar and Flo)...wanted to get married, but she got scarlet fever....So there she was sick in bed upstairs...so the parson climbed up on the porch roof and married Lothar and Flo....And that was a very prolific marriage...seven children!"

On politics: "I was on the Republican County Committee... but I didn't always vote the way the party wanted me to. But don't tell anybody."

On influential friends: "(Pennsylvania Governor Pinchot)... gave us $150 to get Gifford started at Drexel (University).... And (author) Dorothy Canfield every month used to send

$10 to Gifford, so he could have some money to buy some lunch so he wouldn't go hungry.

"So he (Governor Pinchot) invited all the kids, Pop and me and my neighbor's kids to see his slides of his trips to the South Seas on his ship. It was a nice evening, nice refreshments, too."

On hitchhiking to the library: "Yes, I hitchhike and someday I'm going to be on television——the oldest hitchhiker in the United States. After all, I'm 86 and I'm hitchhiking...I have so many repeats...people recognize me and stop. I don't even use my thumb, and they stop and pick me up."

On sleep: "I was told that my house is so old——it's 124 years old——that the mold and the dust...give me asthma. That's what the doctor says. So I said, 'How about sleeping out on the porch?' And he said, 'Okay.' So we put a bed on the porch, and I sleep there every night, until it gets down below 32°. Then it's a little too cold out there."

On writing: "And I'm writing my memoirs, and I'm not using the first person singular. I'm calling myself the Old Timer...not 'I.'"

Gathering Friends from Cyberspace

Some of my closest friends I've never even met! How is that possible? E-mail, of course...and Tricia. Years ago I met Tricia at a writers' conference and Tricia met Robin and Robin met...well, you get the idea. Soon we had a wide connection of friends in their 20's, 30's and 40's—all interested in writing and in staying connected. When Robin told Tricia she'd keep in touch through the Internet, little did Tricia know that she'd be the "O Captain, My Captain" of our e-mail fellowship group of writers. Five years old and 16 strong, we collectively call ourselves *One Heart* and communicate nearly every single day of the year. Some of us are best-selling authors, and some of us haven't even published yet. And how would best-selling authors and aspiring writers come to be best friends? I guess the whole thing probably began with Tricia and Cindy.

Six years ago they drove onto the Mt. Hermon Conference Center grounds in the redwood-filled Santa Cruz Mountains in northern California. They were buzzing with excitement and questions over all that lay ahead in the next five days at their first writers' conference.

Cindy tossed her long, just-permed-for-the-occasion, light brown hair as she jumped out of her maroon Toyota Camry and hugged Tricia, and together they shouted, "We're here! We're here! We're here!"

Cindy straightened her one of many colorful outfits and opened the trunk, lugging out their luggage. They wondered aloud about what workshops to take over the five-day conference.

"I don't know," said Tricia, shaking her broomstick skirt and tucking in her plum blouse. "You sure don't need Beginners Basics. You've been writing for several years now! And your children's books are perfect. Maybe *Writing the Novel?*"

Tricia, now lugging a suitcase up a 45-degree angled hill toward the conference dormitory, turned to watch for Cindy's smile that always filled her whole face. She knew Cindy's deepest desire was to write a novel and loved encouraging Cindy, who always inspired her.

"I want to be a writer," Cindy had said shyly a year before. And when Cindy learned that Tricia also was thinking about writing her own story about becoming a teenage mom,

Cindy promptly took over her *Writer's Market* to Tricia's house and put it into her new friend's hands.

"I thumbed through the big book with all the listings of magazines and the kinds of stories and articles they were looking for," said Tricia, "and I told Cindy, 'I want to do this.'"

From then on they were best writing buds—Cindy working on children's books and Tricia writing articles. And now, a year later together at the conference, they had all those manuscripts with them. But their biggest burning question was not which intensive class they should take or which of the 50 workshops they shouldn't miss. It also wasn't how would they chase down all the 20-some editors of magazines and books.

They had agreed on the five-hour trip there that their *biggest* question was: could God be calling them to write for Him?

Soon they began to meet some of the other 120 writers there, plus the 40-some staff members. One was Robin Jones Gunn. She was on the manuscript critique team and had almost 30 books published. Their first view of Robin was at the orientation session. There Robin debuted in her first of many skits during the five days as one of two way-too-enthusiastic conference first-timers. "We're here! We're here! We're here!" she and her skit partner shouted as they jumped on stage.

As they watched Robin jump on stage, Tricia caught Cindy's eye.

"That's us," Tricia whispered, stifling a laugh.

And as Robin in later skits tried to corner handsome editor Kyle time after time in new and creative ways, Tricia and Cindy again felt they could have played Robin's part. They too were starry-eyed in that magical place of redwood trees

59

and dogwood blossoms and luscious ferns. Could it be real—that someday they'd be published writers?

They also found out that Robin, a real best-selling author, was very approachable. When Tricia's and Cindy's manuscripts came back from editors, mostly with veritable "No thanks" written on their critique sheets, Robin offered to give them some of her own feedback. And surprisingly, she also offered to keep in touch after the conference.

"I wrote her a couple of letters," Tricia said, "and she wrote back, but we still were acquaintances, not friends."

But two years later when they reconvened at the same conference, Robin greeted both Cindy and Tricia with a huge hug. "We just started hanging around with her more and talking with her and some other women there. And soon we began to feel a connection between us."

At the end of the conference Tricia and her new writing friends exchanged e-mail addresses. About a month later, she was reading the book *What Happens When Women Pray?* by Evelyn Christenson (Chariot Victor Books, 1992) when she thought of the idea of creating an e-mail prayer group with her new writer friends.

"I e-mailed everyone and they thought it'd be great," said Tricia. Soon the women were sending their prayer requests and remarks about their writing and family joys and slumps, and she was compiling and sending them to everyone. Sometimes she'd add a thought for the day or a prayer request for an editor or publishing house or informational tips about writing.

The *One Heart* newsletter started with about a half dozen friends and ebbed and flowed over the next year to the present 16 who live across the U.S. and in the Netherlands. Some of us writing friends meet here and there occasionally—at Mt. Hermon, in each other's homes, at booksellers' conventions, in airports, and even in Europe.

And while our initial connection was our passion for writing, our heart connections have developed because we are sharing life together. We shared Marlo's suffering from infertility and miscarriage, and then we rejoiced with her when Bethany Ann was born. Three of us this year had friends who committed suicide. One writing sister needed our prayers when her son was doing drugs and when her husband left her. We often wonder "aloud" in our e-mail: "Hey, just think about what life could bring us in another 5, 10, or even 20 years!"

And we keep each other going in our writing. We help each other brainstorm book ideas, make the right contact, and keep perspective in the midst of repeated rejection. We also cheer each other on when the contract is offered, the book is FINALLY done, and when the UPS man brings the first copy to the front door.

At that first writers' conference Tricia and Cindy both learned that, yes, God was asking them to write for Him. Since then they both have had a prolific number of articles published, and last year each saw the publication of her first book, with many others now in the works.

Several years later after that first suggestion of an e-mail group, however, our writing ups and downs have taken a backseat to our relationships with one another, and we still shout the same cry when we see each other face to face:

"We're here! We're here! We're here!"

I often think,
how could I
survive without
these women?

Claudette Renner

How to Create an
E-Mail Newsletter

You don't have to be a techno-wiz to organize an e-mail newsletter. To prove that, I just started one for my family—and I am a cyberdunce, believe me! Just follow these steps:

1. Open the e-mail program.

2. Give your group a name to use when you address your newsletter.

3. Create an address group through your address book, using the group's name and listing all your members' names and addresses. This will allow you to use your group's name instead of having to list all the names or addresses each time.

4. On the "Subject" line, number your newsletters, such as "*One Heart #1.*" This will help you retrieve the newsletters, should someone want them later.

5. To create the newsletter, highlight each member's e-mail submission, then copy and paste using the Edit command on the tool bar. In our *One Heart* newsletter, we list our names first, then write out our offering.

Newsletter Tips

1. Decide on a purpose, focus, or definition for the group so there is a common connection of some kind.

2. Determine if there will be an upper limit of membership——for example, no more than 10 or 20.

3. Think about a cutoff date for joining the group. Intimacy builds over months and years, and it takes time to build up trust.

4. Make it clear if there will be regular dates of distribution of the newsletter, with deadlines.

5. Make a policy about quoting from or attaching other materials. Remember that creating a newsletter is a form of publication, so you may not be able to legally use some written sources because of copyright laws.

Gathering Roommates

On the best day for autumn color, I was driving over mountain roads toward a halfway spot where I would meet my former college roommate, Katie, for a quick weekend catch-up at a stone mountain lodge. There we would talk and hike and eat great food and hang out in a hideaway with no phone or television or even a bathroom in our room. I had chuckled when I had talked with the reservation clerk a few days earlier.

"There's no bathroom?" I said.

"No, it's down the hall," she said. "Just like a college dorm."

Just like a college dorm? What a perfect place for a retreat with my college roomie! The funny thing, though, was the Rainbow Lodge sounded more primitive than our college dorm! In our freshman year at the University of California at Davis, Katie and I had our own generously sized bathroom right off our bedroom. It was an off-campus dorm, complete with a living room, two other bedrooms and another bath for the three other girls.

We five girls quickly decorated the place with the traditional plants, orange crates, and posters, and fell into the routines of freshman life in Webster-Emerson halls. Sleeping in. Skipping breakfast. Rushing to class on bikes. Rushing back for lunch and the mandatory one-hour block of *General Hospital* and *One Life to Live.* Rushing to campus on bikes again. Rushing back for dinner. And then the

68

evening regimen of Spades, the card game, that lasted late into the night.

I learned several things from that year as Katie's roommate. First, I learned not to be a slob. At home Mom's famous line whenever I asked her if she had seen something of mine was, "Did you look under your bed?" She well knew my routine of cleaning my room was to simply push it all under my bed.

I quickly learned that Katie, however, was a neatnik. She made her bed as soon as she got up. She always knew where her books were. And she hung her clothes up instead of dropping them on the floor. All of that was new to me. And because I didn't want Katie to know I really was a slob, I followed her example.

I also learned that I would never be a horsewoman. UC Davis offered horse-riding lessons for a reasonable fee, so we decided we'd try a ten-week session. We can't remember who talked the other one into taking English riding lessons, but by the end we figured we were lucky to walk away with our lives.

Each week we hoped we'd get the fat, older mares instead of the lean and mean varieties. Things went pretty well the first couple of weeks. The instructor could have put her words on a tape: "Walk. Sit to the trot. Heels down, Janet. Slow to a walk. Elbows in, Katie. Now post to the trot. Elbows in, Janet. Walk now. Heels down, Katie." And so on.

The final, dreaded lesson loomed largely ahead. The whole problem was cantering, really. Trotting is when the horse is sort of skipping around the ring. But cantering is when the horse is taking off—running. And I couldn't control the thing at a trot, so I couldn't figure out how cantering was ever going to work. Or at least how I was going to stay on.

Katie seemed to have things better under control. She just had an affinity for animals. She had lived in the country and had been around people who had horses and such. It was her idea, after all, that we take in Gunga Din. Gunga Din was our schizophrenic cat. He was midnight black and had a very mean streak. I think he hated me. I would be innocently lying on my bed attempting to read some Shakespearean play, and all of a sudden he would fly out of nowhere and land, claws out, on my head.

Katie would say, "Oh, you funny thing" and peel him off my head. I would then leap for the Band-Aids.

It was my idea to call him Gunga Din. I wasn't much of a history scholar in those days. I thought Gunga Din was the Mongolian warrior. It turns out that was Genghis Khan. Gunga Din was the heroic waterboy in the Cary Grant movie that was set in colonial India and based on a Rudyard Kipling novel.

But back to the final horse lesson. It turns out that both Katie and I were petrified of this final session that would certainly culminate with cantering. And both of us really wanted Daisy, the easy-goin' gal who really found the whole horse lesson thing a total bore. But Katie and I were both too polite to just step into that ol' horse barn and claim our steed—not wanting to offend the other by being pushy. So Stephanie got Daisy, and Katie and I learned the true meaning of prayer when we saw the only horses left in the barn were the lean and mean ones.

All I really wanted to do was lift those hooves so gently and carefully and clean all the horse manure out for that sweet animal with that handy-dandy hook and...wham! There I was on the floor again, wondering why I ever let Katie talk me into horseback riding lessons.

But she wasn't having an easier time of it. She had successfully gotten her horse cleaned and tacked and had even managed to get on the 17-hands thing and was clicking him into an easy walk. Seventeen hands, by the way, in horsewoman language is like driving an 18-wheel diesel truck and trailer. Katie could handle a VW Bug of a horse, but not the diesel truck variety. I knew Katie was in trouble when I heard, "Ho! Ho!" Now, "ho" in horsewoman language means shift that diesel truck of a horse down to a stop.

But Mr. Lean-and-Mean had another plan. He knew he had a rookie in the cab and that he could gear up, not shift down.

But Katie knew her stuff. She took hold of her wheel and kept Mr. Lean-and-Mean under control. She would show him who was boss....That is, however, until he put on his brakes and unbloated his belly. And a moment later, the English saddle and Katie were both sliding—and Katie hit the pavement. I mean, the dirt.

And she said, and I remember this distinctly, "Now, why did I let you talk me into taking riding lessons, Janet?"

Somehow we both survived cantering that day. Personally, I've only ridden a horse once since then—my sister's. It took off with me and threw me into a fence, and

I've never gotten back in the saddle again. I've decided that sports that potentially could leave you with broken bones aren't a priority in my life.

There was one other thing that both Katie and I learned that freshman year in the dorm. It had to do with the other roommates. For the life of me, I can't remember their names. That's probably good, because they were a wild bunch. "Rahab" was extremely popular with the male population of the campus, and it was fortunate that she had her own entrance to her room—a window through which they would come and go at all hours of the night.

"Deborah" was a daredevil, a real adventuress. Soon after the beginning of the school year, she decided she would take sky-diving lessons. Week after week she headed off to the college gym and would jump from the top of the bleachers onto mats on the floor, preparing for her first airplane jump. The rest of us were pretty excited for Deborah and wanted to

74

see her jump, but we didn't have a car and wouldn't know exactly where the jump would take place anyway. When she didn't come home, we kind of wondered what happened. It didn't turn out exactly as she expected: she broke BOTH of her legs. It was kind of tough for Deborah for a couple months, because the Davis campus is miles wide, and bicycles were the only way you could get from class to class in a timely manner. She did give up sky diving, by the way. In the spring, however, she took up scuba diving.

It was "Jezebel," though, who taught us our lesson. The UC Davis campus is famous for its excellent science programs— particularly in the field of agriculture. And there were *fields*— miles of them as far as the eye could see. We were on the edge of town, not too far from some of the outdoor classrooms. On a windy day you could even smell the animal barns.

One night we got home late after a bike ride around town with friends. We didn't drink or go to parties or do any of the wild things other college students did. Just being together seemed fun enough. We were pretty uninitiated and pretty naive, actually.

So, when we walked into our dorm suite, we didn't quite recognize the smell.

Katie said, "Gee, I didn't think you could smell the alfalfa fields this far."

I said, "No, that's not alfalfa. I think they're cremating the remains of tonight's mystery meat in the dining hall."

Katie said, "No, it's a sweet smell like…"

And we looked at each other and instantly knew. It wasn't alfalfa at all. But it was another form of *grass*—and the smell was coming from Jezebel's room. And so we learned that while you can't always choose the roommates of your life, you can choose your friends.

And Katie and I have been friends ever since. She lived in Nebraska when Craig and I lived in Kansas. She spent

76

weekends with us and held my first two babies. She went into teaching, and then I followed that path of hers some years later. We both developed a deep relationship with God. Now I'm writing and trying to convince her she could, too.

We spent a full 24 hours together in our mountain lodge that autumn weekend. We hiked mountain paths and enjoyed great food. She read one of my books, and I indulged myself with catalog-browsing. And we laughed and talked and laughed some more. I guess we've learned a lot more about life since that first year in college together. But one thing hasn't changed—we're still very good friends.

By the way, Katie visits us in our home once in a while. And the only grass she smells these days is my husband's real alfalfa fields.

Speak to one another with psalms, hymns and spiritual songs.

EPHESIANS 5:19

Organizing a Friendship Getaway

1. Get all your friends to set aside a weekend or longer time on their calendars.

2. Find a place to meet. Sometimes it's easier to meet in the middle. Someone might be able to offer a home or cabin or timeshare condo for free. Perhaps a friend has a good deal on a tour or vacation package. Make reservations early.

3. If you have to fix meals, divide them up and let everyone help with the planning and expense.

4. Do an information survey to see if the group would like to have planned activities or if they'd rather just talk and veg.

5. Even if activities are desired, do set aside time for sharing and prayer. Take your Bible and journal. Journals could be exchanged to write notes to each other.

6. Encourage your friends to bring photos and cameras. You can keep scrapbooks of your get-togethers and share them from year to year.

7. Indulgences are fun. Take along manicure, pedicure, and facial supplies.

8. It's also fun to take a small gift for each other. Have an early Christmas. Gifts don't have to be expensive. I once found vintage handkerchiefs for my writing girlfriends. I also gave them old photos I had bought in an antique shop. I told made-up stories about my "family" and had my friends believing they were true...for a while! The photos were for the laughs; the hankies were for our tears.

Things Girlfriends Said...

In the 70s:

"Let's go to the mall!"

"Does this mini-skirt make me look fat?"

"You are my bestest friend!"

"Will you lighten my hair for me?"

"That is *so* cool!"

In the 80s:

"Let's go to the outlets!"

"Do I look fat in these leg warmers?"

"I'm lovin' ya, friend."

"I'll get fake nails if you will."

"That is *so* cool!"

In the 90s:

"Let's check out what's on eBay!"

"Does this broomstick skirt make me look fat?"

"Hey, girlfriend!"

"C'mon——let's go pick out tattoos together."

"That is *so* cool!"

81

The endearing elegance of female friendship.

Samuel Johnson

Gathering Neighbor Friends

The most common images of neighborly gatherings are probably Memorial Day barbecues or Fourth of July fireworks displays. In Sierra Brooks, however, the meetings are as simple as one-two-three-four. Aerobics, that is. For about nine years, friends of all sizes and ages have been meeting at their neighborhood lodge for exercise five mornings a week.

Debbie was drawn to the group out of loneliness for girlfriend companionship. She had quit her hospital job to be more available to her three sons as they started into their teenage years. But she found it quiet during the school hours. "I'm one of those women who has her work done by 10 A.M. with the whole lonely day ahead of me."

When the group's organizer moved, Debbie found herself in charge. "I keep the key and write the letters and choose the videos and make sure someone is there." And although the only recompense for her leadership is the encouragement from others, that is enough.

"We have laughed together and cried together. We have shared our faith with each other and prayed for one another. It has been very much a growing period for me in my faith with these women."

Although only a couple women have met together consistently over the years, they've seen many special miracles—and not just lost pounds and inches, but important faith steps. Although the women aren't part of a church or organized Christian group, most have a strong faith in God, which naturally pours out when other women have a need.

Terry (not her real name) was one of those. A member of the group for about five years, Terry had moved to the community after working for many years in the entertainment industry. A standup comic, she had worked alongside many big names in television and Las Vegas, as well as in her one-woman shows around the world.

But she was suffering from injuries from several accidents and the resultant emotional stresses. Terry didn't often really exercise with the women but would walk around the neighborhood with one or more of them before or afterwards.

Wendy found friendship and faith, too. Raised in the San Francisco Bay area, she moved to the small mountain community when she began to suffer from severe liver and kidney problems. Then in her early 30's, Wendy was an alcoholic who had started drinking in her teen years.

Wendy had only been dry about nine months, but the women supported her through her challenges. Several of the times she went to aerobics she broke down into tears because of fear that was overwhelming her from new lab test results. But every single time the women would pray for her, the next set of tests would come out fine.

"It was amazing!" Debbie said. "Eventually Wendy realized that the good results were because of prayer. She saw that God had come through for her." And now Wendy is growing in faith.

Debbie has seen many women come for exercise over the years. They expect to lose a little weight and to get a little healthier. They never expect that they'll also gain a whole new group of friends who'll carry them through some of the toughest times of their lives.

86

Another example is Betty. Betty had grown up in England and attended a church that didn't speak of a personal faith. When the women in the exercise group openly spoke of their beliefs, the light came on for Betty. And then the struggles came—first breast cancer led to her surgery and then her husband became sicker with diabetes and a series of strokes. Eventually the doctors found blood clots in his brain that were causing his confusion that the doctors had thought Alzheimer's had caused. He never came out of surgery.

The exercising neighbor ladies came through for Betty—with flowers and prayers and visits. Even neighborhood women who never attended a single exercise class have benefited from the women's kindnesses. One family in need got a Christmas tree and a package of presents. Several others have had their homes cleaned by the "Merry Maids," as they call themselves. And others have received flowers or meals during illnesses or after surgery.

And Debbie doesn't feel alone anymore. "We've gotten so close, there's almost nothing we won't talk about together." The older women have guided the younger ones in their questions about raising children. They have shared magazine articles together, had lunch out, gone to movies, and been on shopping trips. Debbie has a date with Roxanne for their first mammograms. "It's going to be a yearly event—we're going to help each other through it," Debbie said.

Debbie said her exercise group of neighbor friends has truly lived out the message of 1 Timothy 4:8: "For physical training is of some value, but godliness has value for all things, holding promise for both the present life and the life to come."

"It's certainly profitable to exercise," she said, "but it's better to work on spiritual things. I hope and pray our group never totally dissolves—it's such an incredible ministry. I thought I'd just make a few friends. Instead, God has sent women who have special needs or strengths, and we've been able to minister to each other and share our lives with one another."

"It's not always fun and games. We have cried with one another and hurt with one another. But it's a privilege for me to share another's burden."

In the meantime, Debbie will be at the lodge each weekday morning, opening the door just before eight. You're invited for an hour of aerobics, a season or two of burden-bearing, and a lifetime of friendship.

From every house
the neighbors met,
The streets were fill'd
with joyful sound,
A solemn gladness
even crown'd
The purple brows of Olivet.

Alfred,
Lord Tennyson

Organizing an Exercise Group

Fellowship, fitness, friendship, and fun can all be found in an exercise group. Follow these suggestions to start your own:

1. FORM YOUR GROUP. Find a few women willing to commit to meeting regularly.

2. FIND A LOCATION. Secure a room with lots of space for movement.

3. CHECK INSURANCE COVERAGE. Wherever you meet, check the appropriate insurance policy to see if your activity will be covered, should someone be injured. If you need to acquire coverage, you might check with a local community college or city or county recreation program to see if your program could be covered by theirs.

4. MEET TO ORGANIZE. Decide what kind(s) of exercise you'll do——perhaps even a rotation of activities, such as aerobics for January, step exercise for February, and so on.

5. RECRUIT A LEADER. Even if you decide to use videotapes, you'll probably want a leader to get everyone going and to keep the

91

encouragement flowing. If you're using a public facility, you may also need to appoint someone from your group as a contact person. It may be possible that fees will need to be collected for the use of the facility, so you might want a treasurer.

6. DECIDE IF DAYCARE ARRANGEMENTS ARE NEEDED. Mothers of young children may need the extra support to participate.

7. SURVEY OCCASIONALLY. Exercise needs may change, so you'll want to chat once in a while about whether to vary or step up the intensity.

Extra Tip

Consider prayerwalking with a partner or two several times a week. You can walk and pray at the same time throughout your neighborhood and community. Be sure to notice the needs as you walk along and pray as God might lead you. My book, *PrayerWalk: Becoming a Woman of Prayer, Strength and Discipline* (WaterBrook Press, 2001) provides suggestions on how to get started.

A Calendar of 25 Neighborly Events

January

New Year's Day: Host a Rose Parade Brunch

Martin Luther King Jr. Day: Meet for coffee and poetry reading of African-American poets

Super Bowl Sunday: Go on a shopfest! (The malls are quiet.)

February

Valentine's Day: Sip tea and make valentines—pick up older neighbors

Winterfest: Go ice skating—outdoors or indoors

March

Seed Catalog Party: Plan your gardens or a communal one—bring your catalogs

St. Patrick's Day: Wear green, eat greens, and write limericks

April

Easter: Make Easter baskets for neighborhood shut-ins

Arbor Day: Help each other plant trees, shrubs, annuals

93

May

National Day of Prayer: Organize a neighborhood prayerwalk

Cinco de Mayo: Meet for potluck Mexican dinner

Mother's Day: Hold a mother/daughter luncheon

June

Graduation: Prepare gift baskets for graduating seniors in your neighborhood

First Day of Summer: Go swimsuit shopping—wear black

July

Independence Day: Coordinate a neighborhood parade, barbecue, and fireworks display

Birthday Party: Celebrate all birthdays at once—do a gift lottery

August

Garage Sale: Clean out the house and hold a neighborhood yard sale

Summer Farewell: Take a picnic to the beach or lake

September

Grandparents' Day: Make floral arrangements for older neighbors

October

Fallfest: Take a drive to admire the beautiful fall colors

Halloween: Organize a safe harvest festival for neighborhood children

November

Veterans Day: Volunteer to spruce up a local cemetery

Thanksgiving: Bake pies together

December

Christmas: Host a cookie exchange party or progressive Christmas tea party

New Year's Eve Day: Make your New Year's resolutions together. . .and remind each other all year long

95

Therefore encourage
one another
and build each other up,
just as in fact
you are doing.

1 Thessalonians 5:11

Gathering Mom Friends

"I don't get it, Mom," Heather said for about the tenth time that day.

Sue shook her head. She didn't either. Not the algebra problem she'd been trying to explain to her ninth grade daughter all day in their homeschooling lesson. She understood that. She just didn't know how to explain it one more time, one different way so that Heather could get it.

Maybe I should quit, Sue thought. *Maybe I really can't teach my kids. I just can't go on anymore—it's like a constant uphill climb.*

And then she thought of Redrock Canyon. And Gina.

They had been friends through Girl Scouting before they had started homeschooling their children, but the teaching connection brought them even closer.

"We did a lot of calling on the phone," Sue said, "or e-mailing or getting together to talk through our frustrations. I wouldn't have felt comfortable expressing my frustrations or doubts with other parents who have been homeschooling a long time—you just don't know what they're going to think of you."

But not Gina. She and Sue became even closer when they started taking their kids on desert or mountain hikes near their homes in Las Vegas. "We'd let the kids hike up front with the hike leader to hear everything about geology and plants and animals," Sue said. "We would listen in awhile, but then would be our time to hike and share and get to know each other more."

They drove about 45 minutes west of Las Vegas to the Calico Hills area of Redrock Canyon. The desert seemed endless that February day except it was spring for that area, with the dryness bursting with globe mallow, penstemon, desert marigold, and countless others spot-coloring the Nevada landscape. All of a sudden they were there, in a canyon of red sandstone.

Most visitors to the area would take the leisurely 13-mile loop through a series of small canyons. Instead, Sue, Gina, and the others in their group stopped for a guided hike on bedrock up the canyon.

They were equipped. Sue wore khaki pants and a T-shirt and carried a Camelbak hydration system and extra water bottles. And she also had her typical gallon-sized zipped bag of GORP—Good Old Raisins and Peanuts, with miniature M&M's and Reese's Pieces added in. Gina wore jeans to fend off the cactus and sharp rocks. And they both wore hats—Gina, a baseball cap, and Sue, a hiking hat with "Death Valley" printed on the crown.

Their kids were jazzed about the hike. Sue's children were Matthew, then in sixth grade, and Heather, in eighth. Gina had Laura, in fifth grade, and Christina, in third. They were particularly excited about the rich ethnobotany of the area—how the people who had lived there depended upon the plant life for their every need. They had studied the cliff-dwelling Anasazi people and were excited about seeing real petroglyphs, inscriptions carved into the rock by the original native people.

When they started out on the hike, they hadn't realized how tough it would be. They headed out on a flat plateau about 75 yards, then down a steep, rocky side. That was challenging enough, inching their way down over the gravelly rock, but after they'd gone around a couple corners, the rock seemingly plunged straight down a couple stories.

Gina stopped in her tracks. "I'm not doing this, Sue," she said. "I'll just go back and see you guys later."

Sue waved the kids on ahead with the leader and slowed down with Gina. She didn't want the kids to see that Gina was so petrified.

"Come on, Gina, you can do it," Sue pleaded not too convincingly.

"No!" Gina said, fear mirrored in her brown eyes. "I'm not doing this! You can't make me. I'll wait for you back at the car."

Sue knew Gina's fear was real: her face was pale and serious. But Gina's sudden fear surprised Sue. Gina was the athletic one—trim and strong, a lifeguard who gave swimming lessons. But Sue also knew that fear sometimes had nothing to do with one's abilities or physical strength. And she also knew her friend would feel bad if Sue let her quit that day.

"Okay, here's the deal," said Sue. "We'll just inch our way down, take our time. We don't have to keep up with the group. And…and I promise I won't take a picture of you today."

Sue was famous among her scouting and other friends for taking photographs all the time—catching people at just the right moment with her telephoto lens. Gina gave her a bad time about it whenever they were together.

The problem that morning Gina didn't know was that Sue was also scared. The hike down looked like about 15 or 20 minutes of hiking terror—loose gravel over other rock down a steep embankment into the canyon. Even their carefully placed feet could slip, and the two moms could find themselves eating cactus, at best. Sue wasn't really sure she could make the hike down either. But she wanted to—for her kids…and for Gina.

So she prayed. *Father, I had no clue the hike was going to be this hard today. Please protect our children as they hike. And please help Gina and me get down safely. Somehow I know I need to do this to show my trust in You. And for Gina to see that You are trustworthy. Thank You, Lord. Amen.*

One careful inch after another Gina and Sue made the descent and reached the bottom. There they followed the path behind the hike leader and the kids and saw the red-rocked wonders of the canyon. Sandstone rocks thrust at seemingly impossible angles. A desert tortoise in its burrow. Manzanita bushes with smooth, rich mahogany-colored stems. And the petroglyphs the native peoples had left behind.

They also caught occasional glimpses of rock climbers hanging from ridiculously thin ropes. They had heard Redrock Canyon attracted climbers from all over the world. Geologists also studied the canyon's Keystone Thrust, a thrust fault where older rock was thrust over younger rock, leaving the layers inverted.

The day-long hike turned out to be the high point of their kids' homeschooling year. All the foundational study of geology and history and writing seemed to come together and make sense on their trip that day. And the two friends, who also loved scrapbooking together, found a few laughs when they decided to document their adventure with photos of manzanita berry-decorated coyote scat, which could be delicately described as food remains!

Remembering how she had encouraged Gina that day at Redrock Canyon and not let her quit, Sue picked up the phone and dialed her friend.

"Okay, Gina," Sue said. "This is Sue. Where's the nearest school? I'm dropping Heather and Matt off!"

Sue was half-joking but she knew Gina would, in turn, remind Sue of her commitment to homeschool her kids. And just as Sue wouldn't let Gina quit on the rocky trail that day, Gina wouldn't let Sue quit either. On this bedrock hike of Mom Discouragement, Gina encouraged and teased and prayed for Sue.

Even though Sue has now moved to Tucson, she still is teaching her children, now in the tenth and eighth grades. Heather eventually got the math problem, but she's still not a big fan of equations. She was recently chosen for a national Girl Scouts summer program—probably, Sue says, because of their family commitment to the hikes and the outdoors and the related integrated studies.

There have been moments since Redrock Canyon that Sue has questioned whether her footing as her children's teacher is all that sound, but at those times Sue remembers her friend Gina and how they wouldn't let each other quit. She knows that all moms and all teachers have those times of doubt and that turning back—quitting—is not an option. You just keep inching forward. And slowly, gradually, with God's help and the prodding of a friend, you reach your destination.

*The only thing to do
is to hug one's friends tight
and do one's job.*

Edith Wharton

Meeting Other Homeschooling Moms

Almost every homeschooling mom I talked to said they made connections with other moms doing the same thing through word-of-mouth. Someone knew someone who . . .

If you're feeling alone in your call to teach your children, you could find other moms by:

- Checking a community announcement board. You might leave a notice there yourself if you don't find one that addresses your need.

- Asking your church secretary.

- Looking in the newspaper. There may be an ad in the classifieds or a notice on the family-oriented pages.

- Watching at the park. If you take your kids on field trips, other moms may be doing the same thing. Introduce yourself—perhaps they're homeschooling, too.

- Checking the Internet. Use "homeschooling" + "mothers" as a search tool.

- Calling the local schools or school district offices.

- Asking at youth meetings. Homeschoolers play soccer and other sports, take piano lessons, go to Boy Scouts and Girl Scouts and summer camps. One mom made a friend through the La Leche League.

Balancing Home's Work with the Pleasure of Friends

When I'm at home full-time during the summer and am faced with the day-long demands of my four children, I find I quickly crave the company of adult women. Here are ways others and I have found to keep in touch with other women——even if you work outside the home.

- Let one or more of the kids go with Dad to work one day while you shop with friends.

- Exchange kids. My older two were friends with Penny's kids, also a girl and boy. We'd exchange one kid each for an overnight, and it meant peace from sibling rivalry for one night in both households. Then I could have a friend over for evening tea and conversation.

- Meet for a picnic day. Once a month or week you can agree to meet with friends at a local park for a picnic (or at child-friendly museums during cold months).

109

- Form a housework team. One day each week meet at a friend's house and help her clean while the children all play together. Switch houses each week and your house gets cleaned, too.

- Form a childcare cooperative. Each friend in the group takes the kids one day a week or one day a month so the other moms can meet together.

- Hold a Bible study or book-of-the-month group. Invite friends and neighbors to your house; one of the moms can provide an activity for the children in another room——each one taking a turn throughout the month or year.

- Have a Mom Reunion. Meet for potluck lunch once a month.

- Declare a Library Day. Kids go to storytime. Moms go to their own corner for quiet conversation.

- Take a hike. Let the kids follow the leader—as Sue and Gina did—and have time with your friend.

- Join a gym. Many have programs for kids while you and your friends do aerobics.

- Prayerwalk in the wee hours. Meet a friend before the others are up for a walk-and-pray session.

- Make cookies. In alternating homes, meet with a couple friends and their kids. Form an assembly line of dough and chatter.

- Put little ones in their strollers and walk around the neighborhood—good for shedding extra pregnancy weight, too.

- Volunteer. Working together with other women for a common cause is a great way to bond with them.

- Carpool to sports or other events. You get talk time as you travel to the kids' activities.

- Organize a monthly game night in your home or church. Hire a babysitter or talk the dads into watching the kids. Play cards or dice games for fellowship and fun.

- Hold a movie night. Melissa has friends over for a chick flick once in a while. She says chocolate is mandatory.

- Go out for a movie with girlfriends and their kids.

- Organize a scrapbook day. Your kids' art lesson could be scrapbooking—and you and your friends can get caught up on your own photo albums.

And when you just can't get away...check out the hundreds of websites for homeschooling or work-at-home moms on the Internet. In your search use "homeschooling" + "mom" or "work-at-home" + "mom." You'll find loads of resources, encouragement, and women in the same spot you are.

Gathering Friends of Faith

You don't just find faith friends in church. I met Monica in a job interview for my first permanent teaching position. She was one of the interviewers. The interview was not one of those scary experiences; instead, the four or five women teachers and their male boss made me feel as though I were their friend by the end of the hour.

However, that afternoon was almost a disaster. I had bounced back into town on a hot bus over windy mountain roads with 50 high school students. The only way to survive a hot bus is by opening the windows, and so my fine hair was in sweaty strings. Since we had hiked over Donner Pass trails, I had dressed appropriately, in jeans. At my husband's office across the small mountain town, I had left my business suit, and I hurried there after school to change. I soon discovered, however, that I had forgotten the blouse—and home was 25 miles away, with no clothing stores in town.

The suit buttoned, barely, but left me pretty much exposed. I had planned on leaving it unbuttoned but that was now impossible. A few pounds had slipped on since I had worn it a year before, and so—how do I say it delicately—June was busting out all over, I guess. Craig's secretary saved me at the last minute with a lovely floral scarf which miraculously matched the royal blue suit. I tried to tame the not-quite-long-enough scarf that kept wanting to do its own thing, but I didn't feel especially secure with just it between flesh and the panel of elementary school teachers and their principal. I felt more like a cocktail waitress rather than an elementary school teacher.

The interview went fine, but when I reached across the table to shake hands with everyone, I didn't notice when the scarf escaped and slipped quietly to the floor for its getaway. It was Monica who leaned over and quietly said, "Your fly's open."

I immediately knew what she meant by that remark and found that to be the first of many ribald remarks I would hear over the years from my new friend. I have to admit I was a little surprised when I found she also had a deep Christian faith and passionately prayed for her family and others. Our relationship, ironically, seemed to grow to a deeper level after I left that position three years later and began teaching in my hometown. We then had to make time to get together. My favorite day together was a year ago.

115

"Do you want to go on a reading retreat?" she e-mailed.

"Sure! What's a reading retreat?" I wrote back.

I soon found out. We drove to a waterfall, then four-wheeled up the creek to a spot near some Indian petro-glyphs, which are carved inscriptions on massive mounds of rock. After musing about what the designs might have meant, we munched our picnic lunch, soaked in some sun, and read a chapter or two. In between pages and far away from the sound of anything human, we talked about family and jobs and her dissertation and my writing and God. And every time I've gotten e-mail since then from her, I think of that special place and my special friend.

Another day retreat of recent times occurred sort of by accident—at least on my part. I thought my half dozen friends and I were just going to the mountain-nestled lake for some sun and a swim. When I got there, I found out that the others, who normally meet for a weekly Bible study, simply had moved the Scripture and prayer time from Lea's living room to God's at Sand Pond. I was a hostage of sorts, but what a place to hide me away!

Sand Pond is the lowest of a cluster of pristine lakes that nestle in the gathering of a number of craggy peaks in the Sierra-Nevada range. The whole pond would fit inside the 30-yard lines of a football field, and tall pines stand as sentinels around the circumference. The name comes from the sand that rests there from a long-gone stamp mill that once crushed quartz in the ferreting-out of gold.

We would eventually discover 24-carat ore in each other's sharing and prayers, but some things must always come first! After settling into the best of the tiny coves that scallop the pond and then slathering on the sunscreen, we finished off one of the most important Sand Pond rituals—lunch. Sand Pond food traditions are unbreakable for some of us. I always take licorice. Hannah always munches Sun Chips.

And Pam always squirts her spray can cheese on Ritz crackers. And sucks down her Bugles from each of her fingers after properly displaying them to the rest of the world. It's our one day when we don't care who sees us eat the secret junk food of our lives.

The day had been progressing like a normal Sand Pond day, with a little sunning, a little swimming—you can only do a *little* swimming in Sand Pond—and a little paddling in my Monster Raft. Early in our marriage Craig decided we would start river rafting, so he bought what I still call the Monster Raft. I thought we'd get one for 25 dollars at the discount drugstore. No, we bought one that could do Class 6 rapids—and it cost about half the price of our first car! The local newspaper recently clarified for me what Class 6 rapids are: essentially, you *die* in them or finish them with fewer body parts than you had when you started. One trip over white water in that thing, though, convinced me that

118

ponds were more my speed. In ponds, the rocks don't jump out at you with a desire to bash your head. In ponds, the rocks are all friendly. They don't mind sharing the water with you.

I gave all my friends a tour around the pond in the Monster Raft. What "tour around the pond" really means is that you can legitimately sneak up on people in their private coves and see what kind of junk food *they're* eating. I'm particularly interested in people who barbecue. I always wonder: *Why?* I mean, I go to Sand Pond to get away from the kitchen—why would I want to do all that cooking stuff away from home? My friend Hannah explained that to me. She said it was because those particular cove people included men. And she was right—all the other cove people who were only women were much more sensible. They didn't barbecue. They were just eating their secret junk food.

Hannah is a long-time Sand Pond partner. To me she looks like Julia Roberts only with freckles, when Julia Roberts has big red hair. Her mouth isn't as large but her smile fills her entire face and her laugh is enough to carry me through a whole day. We go to Sand Pond to talk about God and pray, even when we're not kidnapped. Every summer we make our Sand Pond date, and sometimes it has been on or around her July birthdate. One year I took a frozen Sara Lee cake and then couldn't light the candles because of the wind whipping down from the rocky heights. I tried to hover over the cake to protect it from the wind and found out that—spandex does burn!

There's only one bad thing about going to Sand Pond with Hannah or even with the kidnap gang. I feel I go home with more than they do. They have given me a word or two out of the Bible. They have filled me up with their prayers. And

I usually leave wearing a few more hugs than I had when I arrived.

Oh, yes...and they've shared a lot more junk food with me than I have with them!

If I can stop one Heart
from breaking
I shall not live in vain
If I can ease one
Life the Aching
Or cool one Pain
Or help one fainting Robin
Unto his Nest again
I shall not live in Vain.

Emily Dickinson

Planning a Day Retreat

Where to go:

City, regional, state or national park

Stream

Waterfall

Churchyard or garden area

Lake——how about a quiet dock?

Backyard pond or gazebo (no cell phone!)

Quiet ocean beach

Forest

Desert

Roof of a building

Public garden

Art museum

Campground

Cabin

Church camp facility

Island

Bird sanctuary

Zoo

Farm or ranch

Wildflower-filled meadow

Ferry (go back and forth all day)

Country roadtrip during autumn

Paddlewheel boat

Back corner of a Victorian teahouse

Mountaintop

Rest area (some are very nice!)

A camper parked anywhere

What to do:

Take a hike

Make personal goals

Study the Bible

Pray

Discuss great books

Read poetry aloud

Draw

What to take:

Bible or other book

Journal

Filled picnic basket (junk food optional)

Camera (a must!)

Photos to share

Beach chairs and blanket

Table, chairs, tablecloth, the works

Manicure supplies

Cards or box games

Start a Lifesavers Group

Some friendships begin or deepen during the tough times of life. Judy has two friends she calls her Lifesavers. Shortly after she and her husband had moved to Lompoc, California, she lost her third child to miscarriage——Ann Marie, her only daughter. Kathy and Joan had only just met Judy, but soon the three women would bond in a task of sharing Judy's sorrow. Although Joan and Kathy had never lost a child, they showed the compassion Judy needed.

"Many others said, 'Oh, it was just a baby' or 'You shouldn't be so sad over this,'" Judy said. "But they let me be honest——they let me be real."

They took on practical tasks, as well, helping with meals and organizing a baby shower and making a quilt after her third son was born 15 months later. But it was their faithful listening that helped Judy through her grief process. "I know I said the same things over and over, but I never felt anything but incredible love from them."

Judy eventually wrote a book about pregnancy loss, *Good Mourning* [now available as *Silent Cradle: Help and*

Understanding in Time of Pregnancy Loss (Light and Life, 1998)]. "They were so supportive of my writing the book. Joan cried when she heard it was coming out."

Before she moved from Lompoc, Judy helped arrange for a granite marker to be set up in the Lompoc Cemetery, which reads, "In loving memory of each precious baby now cradled in the hands of God." It provides a place where parents can go to pray and remember their children lost through miscarriage. Unfortunately, Judy couldn't be at the dedication service——she had already moved, as had Kathy——but Joan did attend and called Judy to tell her how special it was.

Eventually Joan also moved from Lompoc, but they still worked at staying in touch and now try to meet each summer for a friendship catch-up. In the last five years, the women have met four times in each other's homes for a weekend. "It doesn't matter how long we go between times of seeing each other. We just pick up from where we left off," Judy said.

And now, 21 years after the three bonded in the grief of pregnancy loss, they're sharing each other's sorrows again——rebellious teenagers and divorce. And they will continue to throw out new life buoys of prayer and hope and love.

Maybe you have Lifesavers in your life. Or maybe you are a Lifesaver yourself. Perhaps even you and your friends have suffered the same loss. Whatever the case, getting together for a weekend or a day or even just a cup of tea can help share the burden of the one in pain. Think about starting your own Lifesavers group.

This is God's work.
It makes blisters
and it makes sweat,
but it's worth my time
and it's worth your time....
Working together as
God's people in the world—
I don't know of anything
more rewarding.

Millard Fuller, founder,
Habitat for Humanity

Gathering Cross-Generational Friends

I see a wonderful thing happening with women. Our ages are scrunching together. We don't necessarily only seek out friends of the same decade. This is particularly true when women have the same passion and regularly volunteer for a charity, ministry, or other good cause. For Tricia and Jeannie it all started with a cell phone.

Then they begged half an office and started a ministry that would change women's lives—including their own. In just over a year they would raise funds and inspire local philanthropists and volunteers who would completely renovate a large Victorian home. And Hope House, a crisis pregnancy center, was born in Kalispell, Montana.

"None of us are professionals," said Tricia. "We're housewives, moms, a secretary. But we found that we fit together like pieces in a puzzle."

Tricia was the idea person. "I could see the big picture," she said, "where we needed things to happen." Leona put together the fundraising. Jeannie plans the radio and newspaper advertisements. Ginny does the bookkeeping.

Now they have a dedicated volunteer staff of 40 who run a 24-hour hotline, provide counseling services, offer free pregnancy tests, hold support groups, and give away free maternity clothes, baby layette sets, furniture, and car seats. With the receipt of a state grant, the group has recently expanded its services to abstinence education for area public schools.

Tricia says the surprising thing was that these women—from their 20's into middle aged years and beyond—are now the closest of friends. "We experienced miracles together. We'd have a need for something like carpeting. So we'd pray about it, and the next day we'd get a check for just what we needed.

"I probably wouldn't have become friends with some of these older women—some who have kids my age. But now we go out to lunch and do things together all the time. When something exciting happens—whether it's related to Hope House or not—I find myself calling one of them."

For Jeannie, Hope House filled a hole in her life. Struggles with her own children through the teen and young adult years had left her faith hardened around the edges. "When I first met these young women, I thought, 'Oh, they're so inno-cent. Their kids are so small. They just don't understand what it's like to raise teenagers.' I was jaded and negative."

131

And then she got involved. One woman in their core group of organizers said she had heard that a church in town had a big house available—that a family of 14 Russians the church had supported had moved out, and the church was looking for someone to take over the building for a community project.

Tricia says she only provided some ideas, but here's how Jeannie relates the story:

"We need to make a proposal," said Tricia.

"What are you going to propose?" Jeannie asked.

"I'm going to propose that we'll remodel the house if they'll give it to us rent-free."

Jeannie said she couldn't believe Tricia could propose such a huge undertaking. The carpet was red and the walls were pink or covered with red-flocked wallpaper. There was ugly paneling.

When the church board approved their proposal, Tricia cried and Jeannie thought, *And NOW how can we do this?*

Well, the two of them and their handful of friends couldn't. But the community did. Some groups adopted rooms and repainted and decorated them. Some donated carpeting. They all just pitched in, worked past exhaustion, and did it.

Another woman got the inspiration for an auction and chili feed for the November day they would hold their open house. Jeannie wondered from where all the items would come. "Well, Tricia got on e-mail and took her kids down Main Street and asked for donations," Jeannie said. They made over $7,000 from only 200 items and some chili.

"We never should have made that much money," bubbled Jeannie. "The whole thing just restored my hope. God just kept showing me over and over through these young women and their faith that there is hope."

The ministry hit home for Jeannie when her daughter Mashawn called her from Phoenix. She told her mom she was pregnant and didn't know what to do. "Another time I

133

would have lost it, but I prayed, 'God, whatever it takes, I'm handing her over to you.'"

Christmas had always been kind of rough with the boiling emotions of their dysfunctional stepfamily. Jeannie wasn't sure what that year's would bring. But one of the first things Mashawn got to see when she returned home was her mother interviewed on television about the Hope House. And now Mashawn looks forward to the arrival of her baby.

Hope House has given hope in a year's time to 200 women, their children and their extended families. For Tricia, who once suffered from post-abortion syndrome herself, it has given her hope that other women won't have to suffer from the emotional ravages she has. Jeannie now has hope that her own children and their relationships will be whole someday. And for two friends across generations, Hope House has given them a deep friendship.

For this reason,
ever since I
heard about your faith
in the Lord Jesus
and your love for
all the saints,
I have not stopped
giving thanks for you,
remembering you
in my prayers.

Ephesians 1:15

Rebekah and Pauline

Rebekah, a college senior, has a special friendship that has given her opportunities to serve. She says she can't remember exactly when she and Pauline, now 94, met, "but I know we've been friends since I was little.

"She always made me feel I was the most special girl she knew. She calls me 'my special Rebekah,' squeezes my hands, and gives me a hug and a kiss on my forehead."

That kiss was always an effort because Rebekah, at five feet six, is about a foot taller than Pauline. Pauline loves pretty colors to wear, especially pink, and would tell Rebekah, "Now don't you wear black and gray. They make you look like a storm cloud."

Pauline enjoyed her independence. She was raised on a farm in West Virginia and worked as a schoolteacher before moving to the California mountains to be near her only daughter Sue. Even still she insisted on her own place and lived as long as she could in a senior housing apartment, which she decorated with her cranberry-colored Victorian furniture, old family photographs, and the feminine lovelies of her life.

One day Rebekah was helping retrieve a drink from Pauline's refrigerator and broke a glass pitcher. "There was this big mess, but Pauline just laughed and said that was okay. She was then in her eighties and wanted to get down on the floor and help me clean it up!

"And even though I broke her pitcher, she sent me home with a ceramic vase she had made herself."

Now their roles are reversed a little. When she is home, Rebekah often cares for Pauline, who now lives with her daughter and son-in-law. When Sue and John need to run errands, Rebekah keeps Pauline company. Once she stayed overnight.

"It's no big deal," Rebekah says. "I fix her food and give her her medicine. We play dominoes sometimes, but mostly we just talk."

Rebekah and Pauline have a lot in common, even though they're more than 70 years apart in age. Rebekah is going to be a teacher, too. They both have loved riding horses. And they have a close relationship with God and love "digging into the Bible," as Pauline would say.

Girlfriends come in all shapes and sizes and ages. Friendship knows no boundaries.

One June Day

I had never had one. And I had told myself I would never have one. And then one day I woke up and realized I did. Despite all my efforts otherwise, I had one. A best friend.

I'd always thought it was better to have lots of friends, in case, you know, things wore thin sometimes. I'm not perfect. Maybe someday I'd say the wrong thing or do something stupid, and then I'd find myself friendless. So I've always sought out a wide path when it came to friends——many kinds of women of different interests.

But one day I realized that my best friend——other than my mom——was June. And what someone might find surprising about that is that she's old enough to be my mom. We met through our mutual passion: writing. When I started writing, I went to a writers' group in Reno one night——and she and I figured out that we had met at a women's retreat.

When that one fizzled, we made our own writers' group—— just the two of us. We haven't fizzled since.

138

And then I started reading her my stories over the phone, and she started calling me with hers. And some years later, she moved to my small town. Now if I don't call her by the end of the day, she calls me.

A couple years ago we realized we had another mutual passion: both of us had always wanted to visit all 21 of the California missions that dot the southern half of the western edge of California. Built by the Catholic Franciscans between 1769 and 1823, they were meant by Spain to assert control over the area.

Our mutual passion also related to our writing: I wanted to do some research for a future novel, and she wanted to try some travel stories. So one June day I called her up, and we quickly decided: we'd visit all 21 missions in eight days.

A month later June, my daughter Bethany, and I drove the 600 miles to San Diego and started the quest. Each mission was meant to be a day's walk from the next, although some were never built. Still we found it possible to visit three each day——even with my six-year-old in tow.

By the end of day eight we had visited the most northern mission in Sonoma and were heading for home. We decided, however, that such a trip was worthy of our own awards, and here they are:

Best Flower: Bougainvillea. The dark pink blossoms were everywhere.

Most Common Attraction: Fountains. I have a photo of Bethany throwing pennies into one at nearly every site.

Funniest Janet Moment: When I saw a Franciscan priest walking into the San Luis Rey mission carrying a briefcase. My jaw dropped, and he chuckled at me. Duh. Did I think he should have been carrying a water bucket?

Best New Ice Cream Experience: Oreo McFlurries.

Funniest June Moment: When I showed her how several homeless men were sleeping on the pews at San Rafael Archangel. I think it took her all of ten seconds——enough for three quick snapshots——to tour that sanctuary.

Best Food: Tamales made by Mexican-American women at Santa Ines.

Funniest Bethany Moment: Pigeons chasing her at San Juan Capistrano.

Best Gift Store: San Francisco Solano in Sonoma, one of two that are state parks. We got Russian nesting dolls for $8.00! (By the way, the Russian connection is a stretch; the missions were partly built so that the Russians wouldn't expand a hold into California.)

Favorite Mission: La Purisima Concepción in Lompoc, the other state park. Docents in character helped us imagine the rugged life in the realistically primitive buildings.

By day eight we three ladies——each of a different generation——had learned a lot about that period of California history and a lot about each other. One of us snores, one of us is bossy, and one of us is easily bored. You figure out who is who.

And it was a long time before we ate another Oreo McFlurry.

Volunteering Connections

When you volunteer, you get a two-edged blessing: the reward from helping someone in need and friendships with those of the same passion. If you don't have a friend who can join you, you can count on making a friend anyway. Here are ideas for volunteering your gifts:

- Work at local food or clothing closet
- Assist at a senior center or meals-on-wheels program
- Tutor at area schools
- Read to young children after school
- Volunteer at your local theater
- Help with blood drives
- Fix Thanksgiving or Christmas food boxes for needy families
- Fix a Valentine's Day dinner for senior citizens
- Clean up a cemetery before Memorial Day
- Provide children's programs at a local homeless shelter
- Volunteer for a help hotline
- Assist with horseback riding program for disabled kids

- Visit shut-ins
- Write letters to women in prison
- Offer hairdos and manicures at a convalescent home
- Help at the school or public library
- Work as a historical park docent or hiking guide
- Clean up your local beach or roadside
- Try a short-term overseas mission
- Start a neighborhood Bible club for kids in your home
- Help with church work projects
- Raise funds for charities
- Work at a summer camp on the weekends
- Manicure your city park rose garden
- Send cookie and care packages to young people in the military or college
- Carol to the elderly
- Organize a walk-a-thon for a local charity
- Help with a scouting organization
- Lead aerobics for senior ladies

"Where Two Are Gathered..."

My Kansas girlfriend, Diana, reminded me recently that the most important girlfriend gatherings may not be for light-hearted reminiscences.

"The important part," she said, "is when you have someone from that gathering who calls you at four in the morning, asking if you'll go with her to Kansas City because her husband is dying."

Or maybe another friend is battling depression because her husband has left her. Getting together cleaning tools and taking a dinner may be the best kind of girlfriend gathering you can offer.

And maybe someday you may be gathered, as I have been recently, around the bedside of a friend. She has asked you to come every week to pray for her healing, as she battles the cancer that has harassed her for ten years.

Girlfriends are forever friends when they're bound together with the love of God. We meet each others' very real needs. We love each other, even when we're not feeling or looking so lovely. And when two are gathered in His name, there He is in the midst of us.